MAKE-UP

(E)

(F)

E/. The "Ballerina", a more carefully painted doll; but she breaks PETROUCHKA'S heart.

F. The Dago, from FAÇADE. Without the drooped lids & mouth, this characterisation would lose it's brilliance, despite the excellence of the make-up.

G/. "Chinoiserie": — maiden from L'ÉPREUVE D'AMOUR. The real features of the girl have been completely obliterated with "wet-white", eyebrows & nose have been entirely disguised, & the contours of the face reconstructed.

(G)

H/. The "Faune" from L'APRÈS-MIDI D'UN FAUNE. The ears have putty, pointed lobes added to them. The complete make-up includes matching-up the brown markings on the tights, and softening the transition of a fawn's furry skin into a human being's.

(H)

Sometimes as many as three of these make-ups have to be adopted in the course of one evening.

THE
BALLET-LOVER'S
POCKET-BOOK

*Technique without tears
for the Ballet-lover*

BY
KAY AMBROSE

ADAM & CHARLES BLACK
4, 5 & 6 SOHO SQUARE LONDON W.1
1943

First Published, February 1943
Second Edition, April 1943

CONTENTS

I. FOREWORD

EXPLANATION

The main purpose of this book is to provide some means by which the ballet-lover can identify some of the classical and theatrical phenomena which he sees in the course of a production of ballet. Necessarily, some of the information is of a kind which pertains to all theatrical performances : but, as the more obvious difference between the ballet-dancer and the rest of the world lies in the execution of steps, the portion dealing with classical technique must be the largest.

The *balletomane*, if he will forgive the expression, is like the Elephant's Child, in this respect ; he is full of 'satiable curiosity. Hitherto, the only way in which he has been able to satisfy his appetite for knowledge has been to study furtively rare tomes which he has not the means to buy ; hard to find, they are often couched in terms he has not the means to understand. As it takes two groups of people to form the entertainment of ballet—the artists, and the audience—the problems of the latter are surely entitled to much serious consideration. With all the means in my power, I have tried here to collect the points which represent the leading mysteries to the *balletomane*—a task in which I have had the whole-hearted co-operation of many of his favourites.

I have been warned that I risk running the gauntlet of much severe criticism from those to whom it may appear that this note-book professes to assist the professional at his or her job. I deny with violence any such object, and repeat that my aim is to help the *balletomane* to reach a fuller understanding of the art that he loves, in order that his conscious appreciation of it may be increased. It is to be hoped that the results may amuse, but never offend, anyone who is part of the world of ballet.

Here, then, is a selection of facts made by one who has a predilection for ballet, and a profound respect for those on both sides of the theatrical curtain. "The very head and front of my offending hath this extent no more . . ."

2. COLLECTING MATERIAL

This has been a delightful task. But, added to my existing library of ballet-data, the problem of sifting essential facts from such an accumulation of notes and sketches was a formidable one ; chiefly a matter of separating the indispensable from the purely attractive. The temptation to include sketches of gay backstage dramas (imitations of one ballerina, by another ; last minute costume-repairs) had to be resisted ; untidy action-drawings, conveying in some measure the reason for which they were drawn, had to be rejected in favour of the sequences of diagrammatic dancers which are technically more enlightening.

Concerning the latter ; subject to the strict economy dictated by limited space, the artist's aim has been to achieve a passable accuracy in the sketches which will render the steps easily indentifiable with those appearing on the stage. Each separate series of movements was drawn with the assistance of a proved dancer, and was in each case submitted, first to the dancer who was co-operating, for his or her approval ; subsequently to many other dancers, as well as to accepted critical authorities on every aspect of the subject. Every detail of the book has been through this lengthy process, and in this manner " okayed " for public consumption. I have haunted electricians, risking my life (or at any rate, a fuse) and theirs at the switchboard ; badgered the ballerinas, dogged the *danseurs*, stealthily investigated the sewing-rooms ; taken notes in the stalls, circle and gallery.

I am at home in the theatre, and have always been familiar with the classroom. These facts seemed to complicate my problems,— everything seemed indispensable, yet much had to be left out. I held conferences in restaurants after performances, tired dancers showing an incredible capacity for clear thinking. I nearly fainted with apprehension, when setting off to show the material selected to a world-famed ballerina. But she was enormously encouraging : and I, enormously relieved.

3. *THE SPECTATOR'S RÔLE IN BALLET*

Most authors, at one point or another, seem to yield to the temptation to split the defenceless man-in-the-street into different sections. In recent years, a large and growing section has had to be headed " Disciples of ballet "—which represents the group of people to whom this book is addressed.

This section—the ballet audience—lends itself very nicely to subdivision, and I hope it will not object to being split into two main halves : one half is dressing-room-conscious, the other (rapidly-diminishing) half is not. By the definition above, I do not intend to express what is usually known as vulgar curiosity concerning the private lives and interests of individual dancers : but rather, those people who attribute a brilliant performance to the artistry of the actual dancer, and do not merely accept that artistry as a part of the illusion conveyed by the general glamour of powerful lights and gorgeous costumes ; who do not dismiss those costumes and lights as natural manifestations of the theatre, but discuss designers and electrical atmospheres with equal zest.

These interested people, with their surmises, conversations, arguments and guesses which dissect every possible aspect of ballet, whose opinions I have overhead and noted, are those who have instigated this Note-Book. Sharing their enthusiasm, I have attempted to enclose all theatreland in a nutshell !

To those who may say " Ballet is an illusion, why disillusion its beholders," I would reply thus : " Speaking as a typical *balleto-mane*, I have found that an intimate knowledge of ballet has served to gild the illusion with my greater appreciation."

Consider audiences from an impresario's point of view. They appear unaccountable. Sometimes prejudiced, always kindly, in many respects their discrimination is disconcerting : faithful to a favourite, gracious having witnessed a failure, hospitable to a guest-artiste : often hysterical over a beginner, tolerant to a degree unknown elsewhere in the world . . . a foreign impresario of my acquaintance once proclaimed, " They are always the perfect audience—if only one could make them come ! "

An astonishing fact is the way in which one audience will differ from another. A full house may applaud a new ballet with polite tolerance on one evening ; on the next, the same performance with the same complement of spectators will evoke a furore. That they may vary so much has been proved by anyone who has sat through two consecutive performances of the same film ; an episode which has " brought the house down " in the first instance may pass unnoticed in the second. Naturally, the critic in their midst cannot but be differently affected by either demonstration, and in this way, audiences can be responsible for the quality of certain press-criticisms. They are always responsible for the longevity or otherwise of a ballet.

A last entreaty to the watcher of ballet.—Although there are very many fields to be covered before a complete *understanding* of ballet is reached, the primary function of the art is to *entertain*. Don't be like the lady who said " I *must* see some more ballet when I have read some more about it," and sit with contracted brows, trying to analyse every detail. Enjoy every detail instead, as this is what the choreographer intended you should do. Your instinct will soon tell you if something is wrong : when the ballet is over is the time to start summing up your opinion.

Finally : any curiosity felt by the spectator of ballet is returned in the liveliest possible manner from the other side of the curtain, where daily the audiences' comparative quickness, humour, warmth or sleepiness are eagerly discussed. A fact which, being natural enough, first caused me immense surprise.

4. *TO THE DANCER, THE WOULD-BE DANCER, AND THE ARTIST*

i. A NOTE TO DANCERS

Without your artistry, this book would not exist—and there would have been no need for it. Without your patient friendliness it could not have come into being in this form. I have heard some of you remark, after dancing a gay *variation*, that you wished everyone could know what hard work it was ; if they see this book, I hope they will have some idea.

The material on these pages only concerns you, because it is about you ; it has been accumulated with your help. But if I have unknowingly created any false impression, or am guilty of any outstanding omission, I must then ask your forgiveness. The notes herein come from so many sources,—including some details from pre-war notes, made at Covent Garden and abroad,—that to make comprehensive acknowledgements alone would fill a book twice this size. Therefore, I have not identified any of the drawings with your names ; but the book as a whole is dedicated to you, with every tribute. In itself, it is intended for the pockets of your admirers, to assist them to tabulate their admiration.

ii. TO THE WOULD-BE DANCER

While the following information has by no means been selected with a view to educating the aspiring dancer (—it would paint the career in colours far too frivolous), yet many boys and girls have been inspired to adopt dancing as a career after seeing some performance of ballet ; on top of that, a perusal of these pages may give a false impression. The young person who is enamoured of ballet-dancing as a profession should prevail upon his parents to procure for him a copy of the *Manual of Classical Theatrical Dancing*, by C. W. Beaumont and S. Idzikowski : especially written to acquaint young persons with the problems attending a career in ballet, a study of this book will give them a much fairer view of the difficulties to be encountered.

iii. TO THE ARTIST

The drawings reproduced on these pages show the visible characteristics of ballet in a manner which is largely diagrammatic, and as brief as possible. For example : the method by which the different stages of a leap were chosen and drawn has some relation to the fact that the artist possesses an eye with some of the qualities of a photographic lens when used for action-studies. A dancer performs a leap (which cannot be demonstrated in slow motion) : the artist, having " photographed " it, draws lightning impressions on a sheet of paper without removing the pencil-point from the surface. If something blows across the page, or the artist's attention distracted, the " film " is spoiled and the leap has to be repeated. With the aid of the dancer, the most representative stages of the leap are then selected ; and are subsequently re-drawn in pen-and-ink, with more attention to detail, such as the position of the fingers, and the soles of the shoes.

The value of the original lightning-sketch is partly due to the automatic emphasis of the dancer's individuality. An absorbing study, there is no room for it here.

5. *CONTEMPORARY BALLET*

To consider the position of ballet to-day involves an investigation of the problems of all the arts. Being in itself a separate, plastic art, that of the orchestration-of-movement known as *choreography*, ballet also comprises the arts of music and painting, its aim being primarily the entertainment and artistic stimulation of the spectator.

Its problems are those of all the arts, with certain additional ones peculiar to the art of dancing : at the present day they are increased a hundredfold, but happily they have not proved insurmountable.

While it is obvious that the choreographer is admirably suited to the management of dancers, (he is an artist in the rarest medium in existence), nowadays he is all too often forced to assume the additional rôle of business-manager for his company—a distasteful rôle to him, and one for which all artists are notoriously ill-equipped ; moreover, one that impedes their progress. Valuable time is spent in waging financial warfare, and dealing with the myriad conundrums of ballet-production, connected with pots of paint, yards of material and the personal grievances of scores of individuals. Those should be the occupations of the impresario—who must have a complete knowledge of the æsthetic, artistic, technical and administrative sides of ballet at his finger-tips. The fact that the only other member of the company who possesses this comprehensive knowledge is the choreographer accounts for the latter's frequent enrolment as business-manager as well.

The most recurrent complaint that one hears from the artistic-intelligentsia seems to be " Where are the really great artists : the Stravinskys, Karsavinas, Baksts." It is the same in the theatrical world : where, ask the *savants*, are the really *great* actors. The answer seems to breed another question (for the present writer maintains that there is as much talent about as ever) ; that is—when shall we see another Diaghileff ?

Diaghileff the magician was a phenomenon. He could have no imitators, because he did not lead fashions and phases—he created them, and led those who tried breathlessly to keep pace with him a terrible dance. In himself he represented an artistic epoch. Now, when ballet remains as it ever was, an incubator of innovation, any invention of the choreographer or of his collaborators is often extracted, re-adapted and made common in an evening by the enterprising music-hall. The originator of the scheme may well tire of his idea before he has had the chance to develop it.

Artistic creation is, at the present time, in the melting pot. A fitting successor to Diaghileff will rise to the surface in due course, and gain recognition : in the meantime, ballet is fighting its own battles in various ways, with many powerful and discerning champions, with conspicuous success, and an ever-increasing horde of admirers.

The struggles of art and of ballet are synonymous with those of the whole world—to find a means of progress which is not in itself a decadence. Those who conduct the researches after such a means must trust to the man-in-the-street to differentiate between that which is genuinely a simplification of an ideal, which is progress, and the retrogressive re-hashing of worn-out ideas, camouflaged " *pour épater le bourgeois.*"

6. *CONCLUSION*

To one as prejudiced as myself, anything pertaining to ballet is full of entertainment. Severely technical drawings, however much information they convey, are from one point of view deficient ; they impart nothing of the joy of movement which prompts all successful dancing. Thus, they are very hard to identify with the actions of a living dancer, paragon of accuracy though he may be.

The notes appended to the sketches of steps are not always technical summaries on their execution : this is the case only where such information may concern the ballet-*goer*, the admirer rather than the would-be performer of steps. It is however necessary to pay some attention to technical formulæ in order to underline the fact that ballet allows no latitude to dancers until classical technique has been completely mastered. There is no question of " just jumping about to the music." Which serves to prove that complete individual freedom can only result from an organised scheme, in dancing as well as in other respects.

II. SIMPLIFIED TECHNICAL STEPS

SOME NOTES ON THE FOLLOWING SKETCHES

i. *The costumes*

The half black half white costumes in which most of the dancers on the following pages appear have been devised in order that the separate movements of the limbs may be more easily understood.

ii. *The dancers*

The ballet-connoisseur may think he recognises some of the dancers. He is at liberty to add his guesses to the artist's acknowledgements, proffered herewith.

iii. *The " barre "*

About 3 ft. 6 ins. from the ground, the *barre* is to be found round the walls of the classroom. Sometimes there is a " baby's *barre* " in addition, and further *barres* of intermediate heights for other pupils.

iv. *The methods of dancing*

The sketches do not adhere to any one method of dancing, nor do they differentiate between the different schools (e.g. Cecchetti, Russian, Academy, etc.). They are picked simply on their merits as examples from many different sources, and represent a selection likely to be within the ballet-goer's existing theatrical experience.

v. *Sequence of exercises*

Certain conventions exist, governing the sequence of exercises in the classroom : certain ones have been observed, but no attempt has been made to conform to any one routine with any accuracy.

vi. *To " read " the technical sketches*

Turn this book upside-down and place it on the floor in front of you, when the right and left sides of the sketched figure will correspond with your own.

A.   1   2   3   B.

PLIÉS

Occupying the first page in this book of technical sketches, these *pliés* are correctly placed. Every *classe de perfection* begins with them; every ballerina does a *plié* in her dressing-room before a performance; if you have a dancer to stay with you, he will do them several times a day in his room.

The spectacle of *pliés* being performed in the classroom comes as rather a shock to anyone who is unfamiliar with the basis of ballet-technique: there is apparently no connection between this exercise and the natural grace which the casual observer attributes to the dancer. I have even known a mother to take her child away from a class in which she saw *pliés* performed for the first time: " all that ungainly squatting about, most unsuitable for girls . . ." —she was furious, and would listen to no explanations.

The sketches above show *pliés* in two positions of the feet. The little girl, A, is doing a *plié* in the *first* position of the feet, which is a *closed* position: therefore she may raise her heels a little from the ground, but at the last possible moment. The boy, B, does a *plié en seconde*: the *second* position of the feet is *open* and he must keep his heels on the ground.

Pliés are done *à la barre* in all the *five positions of the feet*. They always precede any other exercise because they soften the muscles and " warm up " the dancer. If a student arrives late at his class, when *exercices au milieu** are being performed, he will walk to the *barre* and do his *pliés* before joining the others. He knows that otherwise he may sustain a serious injury.

---

* i.e., *centre practice.*

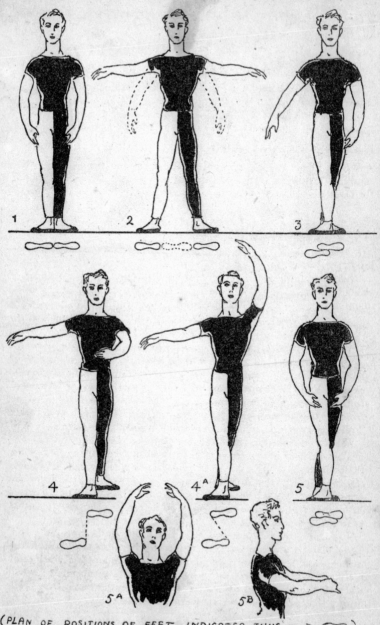

(PLAN OF POSITIONS OF FEET INDICATED THUS → ⌒)

THE FIVE POSITIONS OF THE FEET, WITH THE ARMS

1. 1st position of the feet and arms.
2. 2nd position of the feet and arms (dotted line: arms at the demi-seconde).
3. 3rd position of the feet and arms.
4. 4th position *ouverte* of the feet: arms, 4th *en avant*.
4A. 4th position *croisée* of the feet: arms, 4th *en haut*.
5. 5th position of the feet: arms, 5th *en bas*.
5A. 5th position of the arms *en haut*: 5B, 5th *en avant*.

HANDS : *some observations*

Whilst there are conventional poses for the hands, these may be modified at the discretion of a dancer who is sufficiently advanced for the development of a personal style.

1 and 2. Two views of the hand before it turns *en arabesque*.

3. The hand during *exercices à la barre* : 4. The hand *en arabesque*.

5. A hand held palm uppermost.

6 and 7. Two exaggerated and unpleasing ways of holding the hand.

8. An example of " choreographer's licence." In Lichine's ballet, PROTÉE, the dancers held their hands mainly in this manner.

9. An *arabesque* with the hands simply and correctly held.

10. The reverse: an affected pose with the harmony destroyed.

BATTEMENTS TENDUS AND GRANDS BATTEMENTS : REMARKS ON FEET

In the above sketches, the dotted and shaded legs represent the *battements tendus*, whilst the black legs are raised in a *grand battement* (which last is an exercise for loosening the hip-joint). The white legs are the *supporting* ones. Both legs should be kept *absolutely rigid*.

A. This girl is doing a *battement tendu à la quatrième devant*, then a *grand battement* in the same direction. These *battements* commence from the *fifth* position of the feet. They are two separate exercises, but a *grand battement* begins and ends with a *battement tendu*, although it is performed in one sweeping movement.

B. The young man is performing a *battement tendu*, then a *grand battement à la seconde*.

C. Shows both the exercises *à la quatrième derrière*. A *battement dégagé* is a disengagement of the foot to, or in, an open position with a fully arched instep. On the left, *D*, is sketched an exercise-shoe for ballet encasing a well-arched foot ; the impossibility of forcing the point correctly in an " operasandal " is shown in sketch *E*.

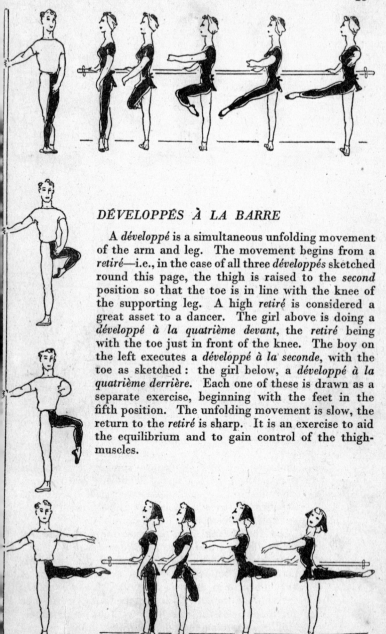

DÉVELOPPÉS À LA BARRE

A *développé* is a simultaneous unfolding movement of the arm and leg. The movement begins from a *retiré*—i.e., in the case of all three *développés* sketched round this page, the thigh is raised to the *second* position so that the toe is in line with the knee of the supporting leg. A high *retiré* is considered a great asset to a dancer. The girl above is doing a *développé à la quatrième devant*, the *retiré* being with the toe just in front of the knee. The boy on the left executes a *développé à la seconde*, with the toe as sketched : the girl below, a *développé à la quatrième derrière*. Each one of these is drawn as a separate exercise, beginning with the feet in the fifth position. The unfolding movement is slow, the return to the *retiré* is sharp. It is an exercise to aid the equilibrium and to gain control of the thigh-muscles.

RONDS DE JAMBE

A. *Ronds de jambe à terre.* The little girl is doing a *rond de jambe à terre* (on the ground) *en dehors* (outwards) : the plan, A2, shows the direction of the same exercise *en dedans* (inwards). An exercise to keep the feet well turned out, toe back and heel forward.

B. *Rond de jambe en l'air en dehors.* An exercise to gain full control and suppleness of the knee-joint. The thigh must be kept quite still.

On right :

1. *Grand rond de jambe en l'air.* Begins with a *développé à la quatrième devant,* and ends with one *à la quatrième derrière* in the case of repetition. An exercise for the balance.

2. *Double rond de jambe en l'air sauté.*

3. An example of *ronds de jambe en l'air* on the stage : the two leading swans in their *pas de deux* from LE LAC DES CYGNES.

THE EIGHT DIRECTIONS OF THE BODY (sketched on right)

(The execution of these positions in class is an exercise in *adagio*.)

A. *Croisée devant* (crossed in front).

B. *À la quatrième devant* (to the fourth front).

C. *Écartée* (thrown wide apart).

D. *Effacée* (shaded).

E. *À la seconde* (to the second).

F. *Épaulée* (shouldered).

G. *A la quatrième derrière* (to the fourth back).

H. *Croisée derrière* (crossed back).

The broken lines indicate the angle from which the position should be viewed, the dotted lines the angle of the foot.

EXERCISES SUR LE COU-DE-PIED (sketched above)

1. A drawing of a *danseuse's* feet in the position known as *sur le cou-de-pied* (literally, " on the neck of the foot ").

2. The *danseur's* feet in the same position, but drawn from the back. Nijinsky, that possessor of phenomenal insteps, is reputed to have said that, in this position, one foot should *embrace* the ankle of the other, as if it was one hand grasping the other wrist. The exercises done *sur le cou-de-pied* are mainly *petits battements* and *battements frappés*, crisp movements to aid the execution of *entrechats*, etc. The tiny drawing shows the Swan Princess's *petits battements sur le cou-de-pied sur la pointe*.

CROISÉE DEVANT

A

À LA QUATRIÈME DEVANT

B

ÉCARTÉE

C

EFFACÉE

D

À LA SECONDE

E

ÉPAULÉE

F

À LA QUATRIÈME DERRIÈRE

G

CROISÉE DERRIÈRE

H

Note : **THE MOVEMENTS IN DANCING**

There are *seven* movements in dancing, viz. : *Plier*, to bend ; *étendre*, to stretch ; *relever*, to raise ; *glisser*, to slide ; *sauter*, to jump ; *élancer*, to dart ; *tourner*, to turn round.

SOME STEPS OF ELEVATION (i)

1. *Soubresaut.* A jump from both feet in any position, with a fully-arched instep.

2. *Temps levé.* Above is one example. It can also be taken off one leg, if the other is raised.

3. *Entrechat quatre.* A changing of the feet in mid-air. *Entrechat-dix* has only been performed in modern times by Nijinsky.

4. *Echappé sur les pointes.* This can be performed by a male dancer on three-quarter-point. Not a step of elevation.

5. 1, 2, 3 and 4, *posé en arrière à la 4ième devant* ; 5, *tourné en arabesque sur la pointe.* These steps are a little *enchaînement de pas,* which means " a fitting together of steps " : NOT steps of elevation.

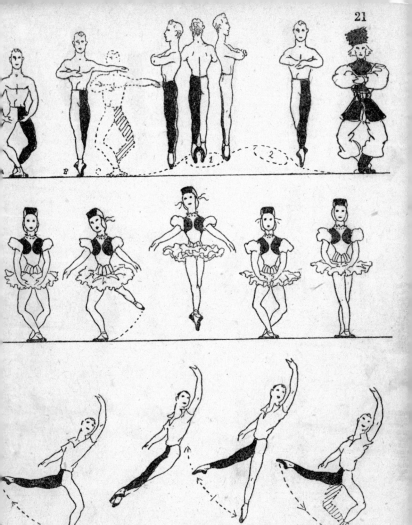

SOME STEPS OF ELEVATION (ii)

1. *Double tour en l'air.* This *pas* is for men only! Turns such as these are well suited to the virility of the Russian *Gopak.*

2. *Assemblé à la quatrième derrière.* An *assemblé* is an assembling of the feet in the air : a preparation for a leap. (Demonstration by Coppélia.)

3. *Cabriole.* The direction of the body and arms is *effacée.* To keep the shoulders and arms correctly placed is harder than it appears. (N.B.—*All* steps of elevation begin and end with a *plié.*)

SOME STEPS OF ELEVATION (iii)

A. *Grand jeté en tournant.* Commences with a *glissade* and *plié*, which is the preparation. The feet should *not* beat (see 4). Example: the *pas de trois* in LE LAC DES CYGNES, act III (see 6).

B. *Coupé, jeté battu.* (*Battu*: "beaten.") 1 and 2, the *coupé* (to "cut"); 4, 5 and 6, the *jeté battu*: 4. the feet

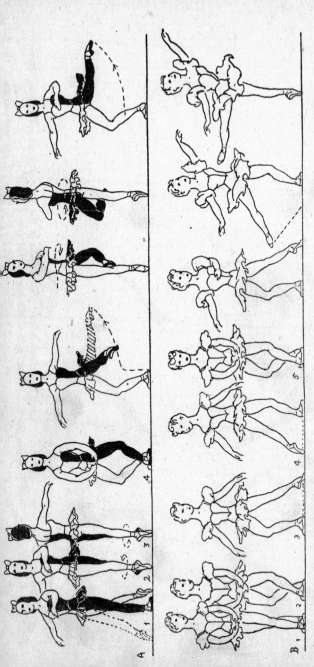

FOUETTÉ AND PREPARATION

A. A *fouetté* is a series of turns on the supporting leg propelled by a whipping movement of the working leg. The preparation is usually a *pas de bourrée en tournant en dedans* (sketches 1, 2, 3, 4). *Fouettés* are sometimes performed in enormous numerical succession by agile persons who have no other knowledge of ballet.

GLISSADE AND RELEVÉ

B. Another tiny *enchaînement*: Nos. 1, 2, 3, 4, the *glissade*; the remaining three sketches, a *relevé en arabesque*.

ADAGIO

The fact that the Italian words, *ad agio*, mean " at leisure," may be a misleading one ; that is, if the word leisure is interpreted as meaning a restfulness to be experienced by the dancer of *adages*. True, the function of *adage* is to give the beholder an impression of a slow and restful harmony of movement ; but this illusion can only be created by the concealment of much strenuous effort on the part of the performer.

At some point during everyone's existence, perhaps when a shoe-lace has become untied, the acute strain of balancing on one leg, whilst the hands and mind are occupied with another matter than that of maintaining the balance, has been experienced. (This example is several degrees more complicated than the " let's-be-a-stork " competitions of early youth.) Whilst tying the shoe-lace, then, imagine maintaining a pleasing serenity of expression, and grace and firmness of bearing at the same time ; when some idea of the physical implications of balletic *adage* will be reached. Slowness in musical time does not facilitate the performer's problems, and many apparently faultless technicians, beloved of their audiences, may become a target for the scorn of their *maître de ballet* when negotiating the stately, remorseless *adages* in the uncompromising and revealing costume of the classroom.

As will have been gathered, exercises in *adage* are usually studies in balance. Well-reasoned movement is another expression for the word, grace : therefore, if the dancer has worked hard and successfully at his exercises at the *barre* and in the centre of the classroom, he need not consider grace as a separate objective. Grace, poise and balance are synonymous, and the dancer who essays an ill-balanced *arabesque* will find himself in a pose which is as precarious as it is ungraceful. (See p. 30.)

In conclusion, *adage* may be summarised as follows ; an *adage* consists of a succession of slow movements, which must be performed with fluidity and an apparent ease, the body usually being supported on one foot. Any monotony is relieved by an occasional pirouette, or more smoothly by a *tour sur place* executed on the flat of the foot. Thus, the transition from one pose to another is a feature of the exercise and impossible to gloss over, as may be feasible in the quicker, more staccato steps. (Action-photography has occasionally rivalled even the eagle perceptions of the ballet-master and rather unfairly perpetuated a dancer in an extremely inaccurate transitional movement.)

ALLÉGRO

It is hardly necessary to state that the Italian word *allégro* means much the same balletically as it conveys musically, i.e. *brisk*, or *lively*. It includes all the steps of elevation, such as the *ballonné, echappé, entrechat, cabriole*, etc., which, arranged into a sequence of steps, usually prove extremely exhausting.

(N.B. Any sequence of steps is known as an *enchaînement de pas*. A fairly lengthy arrangement of *enchaînements* becomes a *variation*,—and here the phraseology of steps often determines a dancer's musicality. The combination of *variations*, with the grouping of moving dancers, and the composition of tableaux, comes under the orchestration of movement, which is termed choreography.)

Young ballerinas...... resting.

1st

ARABESQUES

The drawings on these two pages show some typical *arabesques*, with an example of the *arabesque penchée* by the SYLPHIDE at the foot of the right-hand page. They are numbered in their correct order.

In the classroom and theatrically speaking, *arabesques* are used to terminate a phrase of steps, to give the eye of the beholder time to rest on a poised figure, following a dance in *temps d'allégro*, etc.

A " good line " means, briefly speaking, a good *arabesque* : but it is hard to carry the explanation further than to remark that, from the point of view of the onlooker, when the possessor of a " good line " raises the leg correctly *en arabesque*, the leg thus extended appears to grow visibly in length. *A good line is absolutely indispensable to the classical dancer*—but the possession of it does not, in itself, make a dancer.

2nd

3rd

4th

5th
(en haut)

5th
(en bas)

penché.

ATTITUDES

The first *attitude* was derived from the statue of Mercury by
Jean Bologne. It is in fact an exceedingly beautiful pose—and the
artist feels that it is necessary to make that statement as the
attitude is a headache to the draughtsman ; whose major difficulties
are born of the fact that the knee of the raised leg is held as high
and pressed as far back as possible, and should be higher than the
foot ; thus forming a plane which shows the sole of the dancer's
shoe in startling places. Even when correctly drawn this pose, so
beautiful in movement, tends to look distorted and unreal.

The two young dancers on the left are *de attitude de face*,
respectively on the *demi-pointe* and the *pointe*. Below : A shows a
pirouette en attitude ; B, an *attitude* from a *variation ;* C and D,
two more views of *attitudes*, with the arms differently placed.

A

B

C

D

(SWISH)

1.

2.

3.

POSÉS

Posés are shown here (in the form of an exercise in adjusting the weight of the body backwards and forwards) with a connecting step, 1 and 2, which facilitates the repetition of the *posés* on alternate legs. In the case of the girl, *No.* 3 represents the actual *posé* (which is *en arabesque*). Her body is well placed and she could hold the pose for an appreciable time.

The young man is obviously a beginner: compare his efforts to those of the girl. His feet are turned in (*en dedans*), which is only permissible in character-mime; combined with the fact that he is not paying proper attention to his work, this has brought about his downfall.

A common cause of lack of balance in the beginner is due to concentration on keeping the working leg *only* turned out (*en dehors*), and allowing the supporting leg to pivot and turn in. (The tiny figure is the Swan Princess, who performs large numbers of *posés*.)

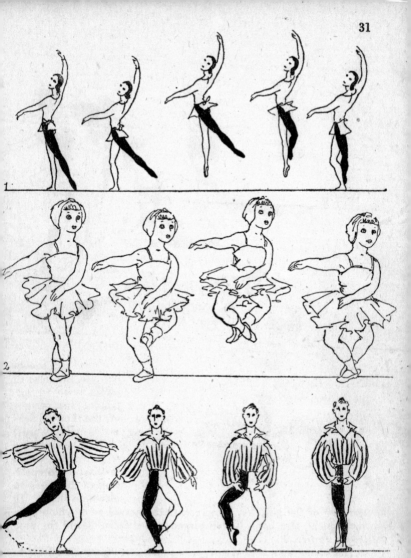

1. *Ballonné simple derrière.* In spite of its name, this step is not so simple as when performed *à trois temps.* (N.B. *Ballon* is a term used to describe springiness in a dancer.)

2. *Pas de chat* (Cat's Step). The assiduous little ballerina above has the right idea and pretends she is jumping over a cushion. This step is performed obliquely.

3. *Pas de bourrée dessus* (over). A gliding step, it may be performed in various manners and directions.

BALLOTTÉS

Having examined the above sketches, it will be readily believed that the word *ballotté* comes from *ballotter*, to toss about. It is an essentially gay step; to preserve the gaiety of bearing and to perform the step correctly at the same time must be a test for any dancer. It is, therefore, a good example from the ballet, GISELLE; which, whilst being full of technical difficulties, also demands great dramatic powers of the ballerina in the title-rôle.

On the left: Giselle and Prince Albrecht perform *ballottés* together.

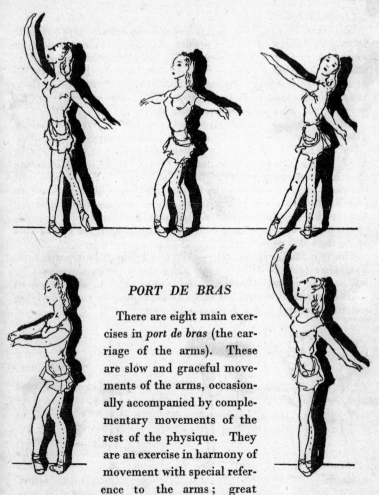

PORT DE BRAS

There are eight main exercises in *port de bras* (the carriage of the arms). These are slow and graceful movements of the arms, occasionally accompanied by complementary movements of the rest of the physique. They are an exercise in harmony of movement with special reference to the arms; great attention must be paid to the elbows, which must always be rounded, and to the hands, which must be simple, graceful and never " flowery." One arm often moves in a different direction from the other, but balances it and moves at the same speed. There must be no suspicion of jerkiness. The movement at the bottom, left, with the arms at the *5th position en avant*, is one which very often occurs in *port de bras* and is known to dancers as " the gate."

" *LIMBERING* "

The very word, " limbering," seems to convey indescribable horrors to a large section of people—(" they break every bone in your body before you are seven " !). Amongst other things, it is affirmed that young children are asked to try to do the " splits "—and that the teacher, creeping up behind them, then pushes them the rest of the way down to the floor. This is but one example of a macabre series of misapprehensions.

On the contrary, athletic contortions take a very secondary place in a class, and have no place at all, in themselves, in ballet. They are not arranged as an indispensable part of a class, or in fixed successions ; dancers often invent their own limbering exercises according to their individual needs. Suppleness and looseness are necessary to the dancer, and she will do her best to sink as low as she can when, for example, she tries the " splits " ; her ensuing *adagio* will be more smooth, and easier. If she has practised her *développés* and *battements* with ardour, she will be able to do the splits quite naturally.

The two limbering exercises sketched below may seem drastic but many feats more incredible than those are encompassed by ballet : the casual observer, merely noting the dignity or wit of execution which results, has often no conception of the underlying muscular control which is involved.

III. THE BALLERINA AND THE DANSEUR

THE IDEAL BALLERINA, in a nutshell

It is difficult to describe the ideal ballerina, in so far as her physical characteristics are concerned : for, although she may possess each one of the definable qualifications of the first-rate ballerina, yet the most indispensable quality is a well-nigh indefinable one. It is most nearly described by the much-abused word, personality.

Up till the time when she develops this quality, she is learning from her art. Ever afterwards, she is enriching it through the medium of her individuality. It is for this reason that it is no compliment to a young dancer to prophesy that " she will be another Pavlova, Danilova, Riabouchinska." The young dancer will be delighted to learn that she possesses some of the attributes of a brilliant and famous ballerina, even that she is such-and-such a type ; but she knows that her own success will depend on her own individuality, not on a fluke resemblance to some celebrity.

The physical appearance of a ballerina must conform to certain specified laws. As to height—5 ft. 6 ins. constitutes the danger-line. On the stage dancers look much taller than they are ; many people pronounce their astonishment after meeting a ballerina socially, " Why, she is only a tiny little thing." She must be perfectly proportioned in every respect and must possess a good " line " (some charmingly-made girls have an unpleasing *arabesque*). Beauty of face, in the generally-accepted meaning of the word, is not necessary ; but whereas a snub nose might not matter, a ballerina with a pronounced double chin, or a squint, would be unthinkable.

Normally, a candidate for " ballerinadom " has been working and training from the age of ten. (If she had been standing on her *pointes* before that age her physique would have suffered irreparable damage, and her chances of success would be nil.) She has taken the risk of growing too tall, but in the case of this our hypothetical ballerina it may be assumed that this deplorable tragedy has not taken place. She must have at her disposal such an absolute mastery of classical technique that it has become second nature to her. In ballet, as in all civilized art, complete freedom of expression is the ultimate aim; this can only be achieved by studying and mastering all traditional steps and conventions. Then, and only then, can the whole business be dispensed with, at the instigation, perhaps, of a progressive choreographer,—who can only express his own innovations through her trained understanding.

It is not only the choreographer's moods to which a ballerina must be sensitive : she must also respond to the moods of music, as well as to musical rhythm and timing.

Many classical rôles demand a great dignity of bearing, and authority she must have ; that usually develops unbidden in one who has had the tenacity to survive the hard, strict routine of classical ballet technique, and, instead of becoming a slave to it, adding to it something inimitable, of her very own. She must be perpetually on her guard against mannerisms, which are often hailed as " character " by undiscriminating audiences.

It is perhaps worth mentioning that there is a rôle in a 2-act classical ballet which, being the most difficult rôle a ballerina can be asked to perform, has become the chief aspiration of every soloiste who wishes to prove herself a ballerina. The two acts of the ballet vary so greatly from one another (—I, a gay village drama ending in tragedy, II, *ballet blanc* of the most ethereal atmosphere), that a successful rendering of both acts has become a sort of public testimonial of a ballerina's artistry and technical ability. The ballet is GISELLE (Coralli and Perrot, 1841). The ambition of every aspiring ballerina to this day is to dance the title-rôle.

THE IDEAL DANSEUR

i. The " danseur noble "

When the attributes of the ideal *danseur* are under discussion, it is first necessary to determine whether one is speaking of the male dancer as a *soliste*, or primarily as a partner to a ballerina : a *danseur noble*.

At one time, the *danseur's* rôle could be summed up quite simply.

He was " the ballerina's third leg." As long as he performed this office reliably, with gallantry and a certain grace, sustaining his partner and an expression of unqualified admiration at the same time, that was all that was asked of him; he was a successful *danseur noble*—of that period. The audience sat, as he bounced through his stereotyped variation, prepared to admit that even a ballerina needs some rest—but awaiting her reappearance with ill-concealed impatience.

Today greater things are expected of the *danseur noble* (although of necessity his bearing must still be chivalrous in the extreme), an infinitely wider scope is offered to him, and his problems are proportionately increased. Whilst possessing a graceful bearing and a polished technique, he must contrive to make his movements seem strong, natural, and therefore manly. As the normal, everyday man's suiting grows more and more stereotyped and severe, so the *danseur's* costume, usually with his tights and big sleeves, grows more and more divorced from our everyday reality, and needs a dancer who is such an artist that he can convey his conviction of movement and mood, whether poetical or merely technical, across the footlights to the audience.

ii. *The " soliste "*

Technically speaking, the same principles apply to a *soliste*; but, whilst a brilliant dancer with a true sense of artistic values will realise the implications of a *pas de deux*, and subdue his own interpretation of the rôle in order that it may harmonize with that of the ballerina:—there are dancers who always appear to remain *solistes*, when they seem to be dancing against, and not with, their partners. This is not uncommonly due to lack of experience in the case of a youthful *danseur*. The example serves to illustrate the fact that a *soliste* who cannot adjust himself to his partner is not a complete artist, whether he is a technical virtuoso or not.

The male *soliste*, in addition to those qualities mentioned in connection with the *danseur noble*, must possess unlimited personality, conviction, a sense of drama and of humour—and an adaptability only comparable to that of the chameleon.

/A   /B   /C   /D   /E

PAS DE DEUX   *Pirouettes, supported*

The girl (who is by the way a little chubby as yet for a real ballerina) prepares for her *pirouette* with a tiny *pas de bourrée sur les pointes* (count "1—2—1—2—1—2" : sketch A), which, followed by her *plié en quatrième* (B), forms her *préparation* and gives her the velocity with which to turn. Her lifted leg is *retiré* and the instep fully forced. Her partner steadies her during her *pas de bourrée*, allows her to turn with his hands either side of her waist, assists her to stop after she has completed the right number of turns ; and disposes his limbs to enhance her final *arabesque*. He must maintain a chivalrous attitude throughout. (See p. 36, the *danseur noble*.)

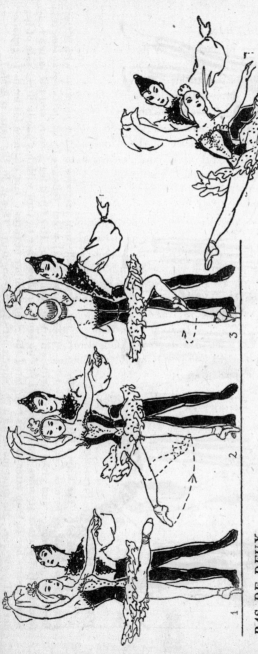

PAS DE DEUX

Fouetté, supported: développé à la seconde.

These two steps combined form a detail from the famous *pas de deux*, BLUE BIRDS, from the *divertissement* in THE SLEEPING PRINCESS, in which costumes the ballerina and *danseur* above are depicted. The *pas de deux* in its entirety is a study in classical virtuosity. On this occasion, the ballerina has to arrest her own turning, her only support being her grip on the male BLUE BIRD's index finger. Compare the poise of her *développé* (4) with the exercise C3 on p. 34.

LIFTING A BALLERINA

With the invention of each new ballet, new lifts are devised. In Massine's CHOREARTIUM, Lichine is carried across the stage at a run, supported by one leg and with the other extended in a real " flying *arabesque* " : an ingenious lift which terminates the 1st movement in a truly theatrical manner.

On these two pages, four examples of lifts are shown. Below is a lift from the climax of the AURORA *pas de deux* ; known to dancers as the " fish dive," the mechanism by which the balance is maintained is usually completely hidden from the audience by the aura of the ballerina's *tutu*. The side view is to " clarify the position."

On the right, 1 : a lifted *sissonne*, from a little-known *pas de deux* from GISELLE, act II. The ballerina's position is considerably *épaulée* (" shouldered ") : it is repeated to alternate sides a number of times. The *danseur* keeps a firm hold on his ballerina's waist. 2 shows a lift from AURORA'S WEDDING : the *danseur* walks a few steps with Aurora on his left shoulder. 3, the Young Girl from Massine's ballet, LES PRÉSAGES, lifted by her lover. Greater strength is needed to lift with apparent ease, than simply to lift a weight. Not the least part of a *danseur's* obligation is to make his ballerina appear as light as the immortal Sylphide herself, and to raise her with no apparent effort.

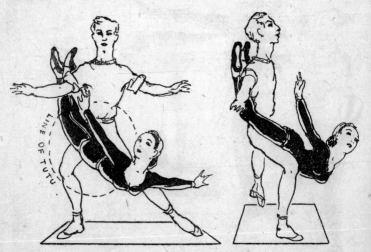

IV. MISCELLANEOUS NOTES

CHARACTER AND DEMI-CARACTÈRE

Even as there is an exception to prove every rule, so the existence of character-dancing and mime in ballet goes to disprove every stipulation of classical technique. (For example: a character-turn, to put it briefly, implies a *pirouette* performed *en dedans*, with the feet *en dedans* (" turned in ")—an unheard of phenomenon outside a character-class.) Of course, character and classical ballets are not by any means kept in watertight compartments; Hilarion, a most sinister villain and a purely character rôle, disturbs the otherwise impeccable classicism of the *ballet-blanc* from GISELLE, act II. Apart from this amalgamation, there is *demi-caractère*, which, as the name implies, is something between classical dancing and character-mime. A survey of the theatrical appeal of ballet when it is purely classical will perhaps assist us to define the meaning of the terms character and *demi-caractère*. A rôle which is composed of undiluted classicism, such as that of Princess Aurora, imparts to the audience the superb results of the dignity of classical training : a training which makes of a *pas de deux* a drama of muscular and emotional restraint, which constitutes a thrill in itself, a theatrical *tour de force*. The success of such a ballet depends upon the technical brilliance of the dancers ; without that, little remains to hold the attention. Whilst the audience, as a whole, may feel the current excitement, the genuine thrill of appreciation is for that mixture of connoiseur, critic, artist and madman—the balletomane.

In a character or *demi-caractère* ballet, the appeal is more obvious, and may be treated with more brevity. There is usually a definite plot ; or gay costumes, at least, from which the audience may feel a familiar warmth, a *reconnaissance de lieu*. A character-dance is usually taken to mean a dance in which *les pointes* are not used : or a national dance of some kind. Lifts, technically speaking, are not used in character-ballet. A *demi-caractère* rôle is taken to be one in which the *pointes* may be used, but in which an ability for characterisation, or dramatic power, is demanded of the dancer.

N.B.—With regard to Symphonic Ballet (the critic's bone of contention) : Massine's CHOREARTIUM has no plot, the *pointes* are used, lifts are employed in great numbers, and from those points of view it should therefore be a classical ballet. Nevertheless, it is an interpretation of the moods of Brahms's music, which are so highly dramatic that, accompanied by excellent parallels in movement, the result can be most nearly described by a contradiction in terms : viz., a *melodrama without a plot*.

Character ballets are often appropriated, as it were, by the dancer who first interprets the leading rôle : much indifferent choreography may appear successful, when created especially to exploit the gifts of a certain *artiste* : unhappy is his successor, who will always be unfairly compared with the original performer.

PETROUCHKA is surely the most outstanding example of a character ballet : the perfect dance-drama. First presented in 1911, with Nijinsky in the title-rôle, it also represents the ideal collaboration between choreographer, composer and artist ; respectively M. Fokine, I. Stravinsky, and A. Benois. In spite of the definition, that character ballet is performed without the use of the *pointes*, one of the puppets in PETROUCHKA dances on her toes—the *Ballerina* ; her laborious adagio, stiffly accompanied by the ponderous Moor, is a masterly caricature of classical technique which invariably provokes appreciative chuckles from the young dancers to be found in every ballet-audience.

Another perfect example of a character-ballet is Massine's tribute to Spanish dancing, LE TRICORNE ; this time, no lifts, no *pointes* ; proving the rule that, when based on some form of National Dancing, a ballet may nearly always be described as being " character."

A further example is the *period* ballet, of which a particularly fine example is THE RAKE'S PROGRESS, with choreography by Ninette de Valois.

With regard to *demi-caractère* : ballet of this description covers an enormous range of period, nationality, and mood. LE BEAU DANUBE, a mixture of gaiety and nostalgia which is such an excellent parallel for the music of Johann Strauss, with sympathetic *décor* by V. Polunin, is a masterpiece of Massine's. Equally successful is Ashton's LES PATINEURS ; the perfect harmony of William Chappell's *décor* and costumes, Meyerbeer's infectious music, combined with a certain wit in details of the choreography, tends to camouflage a perfection of general pattern for which, as always, Frederick Ashton should be paid especial tribute. In his handling of groups he stands alone. LES PATINEURS may be a *demi-caractère* ballet ; it will have its place in the classics.

APPRECIATION OF THE DANCER

The material in this pocket-book deals with a selection of the strictly material aspects of the art of ballet. Scantily-clad gnomes demonstrate a few steps ; an exasperated little ballerina scrambles angrily after her truant cotton-reel—normal occurrences in the lives of apparently ordinary beings ; yet without the dancers' exceptional capacity for endurance and hard work, the choreographer would be as powerless as an artist with no palette, paint or canvas. The impulse which impels them to work as they do, for what is in a worldly sense an infinitesimal reward, has not been indicated in the slightest degree. To attempt to encompass the æsthetic dancers' point-of-view in this tiny space is so impossible a task, that perhaps it is unwise to broach the subject ; it would have to be so summarily treated that dancers may receive the impression that their problems and aims are underestimated, and this would be an injustice to the writer.

It is perhaps unnecessary to explain the passionate love of the ballet-dancer for her art, to the balletomane, who shares it ; thus doing almost as much as the dancer for its survival. Proof of the dancer's devotion, if needed, can be found in the fact that most of them are sadly, if necessarily, underpaid ; that their rigorously trained limbs and intelligences render them extremely suitable for presentation on the vaudeville stage, and the like ; and I have known two dancers, left literally stranded and without money owing to cancellation of engagements at the outbreak of war, write cryptic and scornful refusals on the frenzied, reply-paid telegrams sent, offering them contracts at terms which exceeded the wildest dreams of the ballet-world, by an extremely famous variety-impresario.

The immoderate love of the ballet-dancer for her art does not necessarily fluctuate, unfortunately, according to her talents. Some dancers, who seem to have cherished the ambition to dance even before they knew the meaning of the word, who have worked and toiled under the best teachers and conditions, have not made successful artists. This is bitter tragedy for the dancer. Conversely, there are those who, having all the natural gifts of the first-rate dancer, with a brilliant future before them, lack the flame of ambition, and only give a taste of their powers when their indolence allows it ; that is tragedy for the balletomane.

TRIBUTE TO CHOREOGRAPHERS

A recipe for ballet : *Take 1 choreographer, 1 composer and 1 artist : add a sprinkling of criticism, a little heated conversation, and set the mixture in a congenial atmosphere to cool, when ideas will soon be seen to rise to the surface.*

Whatever the subject of a ballet, whatever its object, the ideal circumstances for its construction remain the same. It consists of the pooling of the resources of a choreographer, a composer, and an artist : the addition of a sympathetic and knowledgable " chairman," to catch and control fleeting ideas, is an advantage : the complete success of the resulting ballet may be said to depend as a whole upon the theatrical value of the initial idea, and upon whether the subsequent translations of them into terms of movement, colour and musical composition will harmonize with one another, resolving themselves into a plastic whole which is pleasing and artistically stimulating.

It is very hard to cater for the ballet-audience of today. A considerable percentage of it consists of self-appointed critics— very harsh ones, at that. They come to see what may be described as Progressive Ballet, and the more obscure the theme, the more tangled the arms and legs, the better. An even larger percentage is termed the up-to-town-for-the-day family (" We will go to such-and-such a ballet, it will be nice to be able to say we've seen it.")

The choreographer's field of action is an enormous one : very many reasons may prompt him to create new works, and enlarge the horizon even more for artists. If the work incorporates a completely new idea, the excitement before its presentation is electric ; but its first reception is often completely at variance with its ultimate success. THE SLEEPING PRINCESS was a mis-calculated revival of Diaghileff's audience : it was too great an anticipation of their taste, and proved an enormously expensive failure. Now it is one of the chief attractions of the Sadler's Wells Ballet. L'APRÈS-MIDI D'UN FAUNE was a *succès de scandale* : now it is performed comparatively seldom. Symphonic ballet, the first example of which was LES PRÉSAGES to Tchaikowsky's fifth symphony, created an unprecedented theatrical battlefield ; some hostilities are still in progress : but choreographers, prompted by their innate muscular reaction to the changing moods of symphonic splendour, are responsible for much of the present-day love and understanding of the great composers.

Ballet is popular as never before, it is on view in an incredible number of theatres, playing to amazingly large audiences. Never-theless, the self-appointed critics appear to be in their element, and pour a stream of acrid letters into the various managements. But the general opinion of the sort of people who know instinctively the value of an idea and of a cause, who upon occasion pretend to like margarine better than butter or to prefer saccharine to sugar, is the opinion which can make a production famous : i.e., the " nose " of the ordinary public for *good theatre*.

V. OBSERVATIONS ON COSTUME

INTRODUCTORY

The interested observer of ballet is bound to feel a certain curiosity concerning some aspects of the conventional costumes. This section constitutes a necessarily brief attempt to elucidate some of the major mysteries : but it does not profess to assist the professional, or to be anything but a superficial survey of one of the highly complicated mechanisms pertaining to the theatre.

Such information as there is room to include herein may prove of use, however, to the amateur costume designer (who so often fails to recollect that the wearer must get *into* the costume somehow !—and then, dance in it). Most of the following details have been selected in response to the queries most prevalent amongst ballet-audiences. One lady, loading her sympathies on to the dancers, avowed to her companion that the poor things were in a terrible way for shoes—" why, look through these glasses, there's not one of those girls but has her shoes darned so's you can almost see the stitches."

She was quite right, and today shoes are indeed a terrible problem : but the explanation of the darning appears on one of the following pages.

Other chance remarks, repeatedly overheard ; questions continuously asked, such as " why don't they wear something *pretty* to practise in " ; demands from anxious ballet-mammas, how to make the budding ballerina's skirt " stick straight out,"—all these

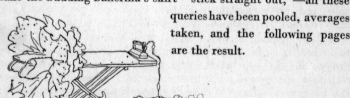

queries have been pooled, averages taken, and the following pages are the result.

ROMANTIC TUTU

The *Romantic Tutu* has a basque, like the classical one (see following pages), but it is hidden and the visible bodice finishes at the waist. There are usually three frills in all; the top one being gathered into the waist, and the other two are sewn one below the other onto the tarlatan basque, which prevents bulkiness. The bodice is generally made of slipper-satin, and small wing-like sleeves are added to the shoulder-straps, which are of elastic encased in satin. The top frill and the sleeves are sometimes made of material less coarse than the tarlatan, such as stiffened net or organdie. The edges of all tarlatan skirts are occasionally pinked. The length of the *romantic tutu* from waist to hem is usually about 30 ins.; in the event of a *corps de ballet* of varying heights, all the skirts are arranged so that they are about 9 ins. above the floor.

SLEEVE

CLASSICAL TUTU (i)

A phenomena which seems to puzzle a large number of balleto-manes is the mysterious way in which the classical *tutu* is induced to " stick out " so stiffly.

The incomparable frothiness of the ballet skirt is not due to the use of an immoderate amount of material (amateurs generally employ too many frills of too great a length) : it is due to the way in which the frills are graded, the manner in which they are distributed on a close-fitting base and, in some cases, the enterprising introduction of a light, crinoline-wire hoop.

The sketch on this page shows two views of a straightforward classical *tutu*, and a decorated over-dress on a hanger.

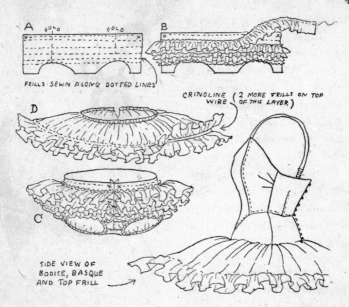

FRILLS SEWN ALONG DOTTED LINES

CRINOLINE WIRE (2 MORE FRILLS ON TOP OF THIS LAYER)

SIDE VIEW OF BODICE, BASQUE AND TOP FRILL

CLASSICAL TUTU (ii)

The foundation of the *Classical Tutu* is a pair of " briefs " cut all in one piece, out of tarlatan (diagram A). Important—the frills are sewn on before the seams of the briefs are joined up. Each frill is made from three widths of the 36-in. material ; the bottom frill is 1½ ins. deep, the next four respectively 2½ ins., 4 ins., 5 ins. and 6 ins. (see B). The briefs are then sewn up and elastic inserted in the legs (C). Then, two wider frills between which is enclosed the circle of crinoline-wire (this is what keeps the *tutu* sticking straight out (D)) ; then four layers of frills on top of that. The topmost frill is usually decorated with swansdown and sequins for the Swan Princess, gay ribbons for Coppélia, etc. This *tutu* is attached to a basque which starts at the wearer's natural waist, and varies in depth from 4 ins. to 6 ins. ; it should fit tightly to the hips. It would undoubtedly ride up were it not for the pants underneath. The bodice is usually supported by shoulder-straps of elastic, with pearls or other decoration sewn on.

COSTUMES OF THE DANSEUR

Having touched upon the essential details of the ballerina's *tutus*, it seems only fair to add a page concerning the costumes of the *danseur*. On the right is a selection from his wardrobe: *A*, an example of the Greek *chiton*; *B*, the generally accepted classical costume—a velvet jerkin, and tights; *C*, the black velvet *gilet*, white silk shirt and white tights from the famous male rôle in LES SYLPHIDES.

Whilst the latter costume nearly always remains the same, apart from some fluctuations in the colour and arrangement of the wig, the first two are subject to some variation in every particular. The *chiton*, which is usually adopted to portray some such personage as Icarus, Orpheus, or Paris, consists as a rule of a short white pleated kilt, set off by the very brown limbs of the wearer. The upper part of the costume may include, e.g., a cape, or draperies, and/or wings.

The costume, *B*, nearly always retains the same silhouette; the latitude of the designer usually being in the choice of colour and decoration.

TIGHTS

However effectively costumes are designed, however exquisitely carried out, they will make but a poor show if the wearer's tights are not as a second skin. Stage lighting is a fine exaggerator of folds and wrinkles, a fact that has been proved all too often by the appearance of the heroes of pantomime—and of opera.

The ballet, collectively, seems to have solved the problem. The writer has been asked to elucidate. With the information that the more often tights are washed, the better they fit, it is to be hoped that sketches 1 and 2 on the right will help to clear up the matter.

BLOCKED SHOES

These appear to constitute another mystery to a number of ballet-lovers. Sketch 3, *A*, at the bottom of the page shows a new ballet-shoe darned and ready for use. The purposes of darning are mainly to prolong the life of the shoe, to " grip " the floor more safely, and to lessen the contact between a hard floor and the toes. Landing on the *pointes* is in itself neither painful nor difficult. The dotted line on sketch *A* indicates the part of the shoe that is stiffened i.e., the " block."

UNFLATTERING COSTUMES

These sketches serve to show some of the ways in which a perfectly-proportioned figure may suffer, if the costume does not lend itself to the movements of dancing.

In sketch A the girl appears to suffer from a short neck and hunched shoulders: B shows a more becoming reconstruction. C, " body-tights "; when worn alone they ill become the masculine figure. D shows the Red Knight from CHECKMATE, where cleverly-embellished body-tights have been used with success. E shows a *tutu* with the bodice cut to flatten, rather than to flatter, the figure ; the basque too deep, the *tutu* overpowering and dowdy.

F shows the costume more pleasingly executed: G shows the unfortunate results if the top of the *danseur's* tights are decorated to represent breeches ; the sleeves do nothing to counterbalance heaviness of the lower part of the costume. A " V neck " completes the effect of this attire, which I have invented in order to horrify the balletomane.

PRACTICE COSTUME

The severity of the usual practice dress is devised to reveal the dancer's movements to the utmost. The bent knee, the relaxed *pointe*, are immediately noted and condemned by the *maître de ballet*. Hair is usually tied back—a fuzz of curls round the face may mask an incorrectly placed head. The dancers sketched above are in the motley dress necessitated by clothes-rationing problems. The generally accepted dress is worn by the figure marked X.

1. RUSSIAN

The girl below is wearing one of the costumes by Gontcharova for the ballet YGROU-CHKA. Her sandals are made to resemble straw *valinki*. The man wears the type of costume usual in dancing the *Gopak*. (Music by Rimsky-Korsakov).

2. SPANISH

Argentina's dancing was admired by balleto-manes: her country's dances have influenced ballet. The costumes below are after Picasso's designs for LE TRICORNE —Massine's translation of his knowledge of Spanish dancing into terms of ballet. (Music by de Falla).

3. POLISH

Two costumes from CRACOW WEDDING, these are examples of Polish national dress that need no readjustment for the gay type of dance that is performed in them— mostly variations of the mazurka-time so dear to Polish composers.

4. SCOTTISH

Costumes from THE TARTANS, choreographer Frank Staff. It is hard to be original with plaids and tartans, but these costumes are witty and unmistakably Scottish without resort to banality. (Music by Boyce. Costumes by William Chappell).

5. ORIENTAL

Directly below is the usual costume for the Egyptienne from CASSE-NOISETTE. Lower down, the Golden Slave from the colourful SCHÉHÉ-RAZADE, his costume gold, his skin painted silvery. (Costumes by Bakst. Music by Rimsky-Korsakov).

6. "CHINOISERIE"

The hero and heroine from Fokine's ÉPREUVE D'AMOUR. Chinoiserie at its most engaging. Costumes by Derain. Music: Mozart's idea of what the Viennese court's idea of China would be like. . . .

This is a sketch made from a small theatre, and the reader must also make allowances for the artist's lack of space. The arrow, 1, indicates one or more swinging spotlights operated from high up behind the audience (or, in the case of a large theatre, from a crow's nest in the dome of the roof). 2, A batten on a movable pulley; 3, 4 and 5, large swinging arcs. There are usually several layers of these and a silhouette effect may be obtained by lowering a screen between them. Here they are sketched much lower than they should be. 6 and 7, two specimens of large unfixed spotlights; 8 and 9, two squat floodlights; 10, footlights; 11, stage-manager's signal-bulb; 12, the switchboard—very complicated, the mechanism extends underneath the stage, and governs the entire system of lighting; 13, some of the coloured filters for the spots; 14, one of a warren of diminutive trap-doors whereby the electric flex connects the lamps with the current below stage. (*See overleaf for further notes on lighting*.)

N.B.—The ballerina is using the rosin-box, for safer " turning."

VI. NOTES ON THEATRICAL LIGHTING *

The sketch of a normal but much simplified arrangement of stage lighting has a place in this book, because so very much depends upon illumination, although most people are inclined to take it for granted. Upon the occasions that the artistic mammoth, Diaghileff, was asked " what he actually *did* " in connection with his ballet, it is reported that he always replied " You can say I supervise the lighting." Although this is a triumph of under-statement, still—had he been speaking no less than the truth, it would have stood for a good deal. Theatrical lighting is a highly specialised science, both in the artistic and purely technical sense.

It is the producer's job to reproduce as nearly as possible an artificial atmosphere which will ensure that the *décor* and costumes will retain the colours depicted on the artists' original designs ; at the same time, the arrangement of lighting must not be one which will play unintended tricks of colour and shadow on the faces of the dancers. When a back-cloth has been much battered and creased during a tour, the stage-manager must patiently seek a combination of the mobile lights, dimming some and opening up the others, whereby the illusion of a perfect surface is created. The chief electrician must know every ballet by heart, and bully his staff into perfect team-work ; must see that they are quick, quiet and alert ; must keep a weather-eye on the stage-manager, be ready to respond immediately to his frenzied signals.

In a large opera-house, a whole telephone-and-signal system connects the different electrical departments : there may be as many as five " stories " of platforms, each with spotlight and operator, connected by step-ladders and telephones, behind either side of the proscenium ; and a whole suspended passageway of floating lights shining down from above the footlights, many scores of feet above the stage, complete with its gangway, staff and telephone.

---

* These notes concern the characteristics of various touring ballet-companies, and must not be taken as an account of the conventions of general theatrical staffs.

VII. WARNINGS FOR THE BALLET-LOVER

1. *If you are keen to experience a little dancing yourself :*

    a. If it's just for fun, don't buy a pair of block shoes and romp about on them with your knees bent. You'll probably break one of your big toes.

    b. If you are more serious, remember that the blocks are there to *assist* you to stand on your toes : don't expect them to do all the work for you. Strengthen your feet with exercises *à la barre.*

    c. If you are under ten years of age, *don't stand on your toes at all.* You might do yourself such damage that you will never become any sort of a dancer.

2. *If you are interested in elevation :*

    a. Don't essay a leap " just to see how they do it " without working up to it first with *pliés,* then with the action in slow motion.

    b. Make sure that your leaping experiments are not upon too hard a surface. Some wood can be hard and unyielding (and beware also against slipperiness). Grass lawns in summer are a menace, the grass itself has a misleading softness which may camouflage hard baked earth, and a danger of severe injury to spine or groin.

    c. If you wish to investigate the intricacies of some step of elevation, do so first sitting on a solid piece of furniture. If you jump with enthusiasm, and land on the side of your foot, trouble will follow.

    d. In the event of experimental *pirouttes* with a friend, mind your finger-nails, or cut them—you don't want a partner with only one eye. . . .

3. *If you are a " ballet-mamma,"* the importance of 1. *c.* above can scarcely be overstated. It is most likely that you will have to withstand the heartrending entreaties of the little *ballerina* herself, who will assure you that a refusal to provide a pair of the lovely pink satin blocked slippers will result in her early decease ! Occasionally, in the case of a child with exceptional talent, it has been known that unprincipled persons, advertising themselves as teachers of ballet, have seen in the child a further supply of laurels for themselves, and have forced her unmercifully in her career from purely selfish motives. Obviously, the final results have been shocking for the child. The mother must be on her guard, then, against plausible flattery.

4. *If you are admitted backstage during a performance :*

    a. Never kick a curtain. They have enormously heavy metal " shoes " hidden in their folds, to keep them from billowing out in the draught for which all theatres are famous. A blackened toe-nail would be your souvenir.

    b. Never lean your full weight against anything. Solid-looking pillars, brick walls, etc., often prove to be painted canvas on a frame.

5. *Finally—an entreaty to admirers.* If you wish to give a ballerina a bouquet of roses, you are besought to see that the larger thorns are removed, or covered. Remember that her arms are usually uncovered ; when she embraces a large sheaf of roses handed to her by the attendant, if the stalks have not been de-prickled, the results may be better imagined than described.

VIII.   TAKING A CALL

Every ballerina forms her own personal way of acknowledging her applause.   The sketches above are not intended to deal with this individual aspect of an obeisance, but can be described as follows :   *A* may be said to represent the romantic curtsey ;   *B*, the classical " bow."   The manner in which both the ballerina and the *danseur* make their bows varies with the nature of the ballet.

INDEX

GARGOUILLADE

A FINAL HEADACHE FOR THE BALLET-GOER

TWO DEFINITIONS : 1. "You gargle with your feet" (from an expert in ballet).

2. "You do so much with your feet that you don't know what you've done" (from a dancer).

The step is composed of a *double rond de jambe en l'air, en dedans* with the first leg, *en dehors* with the second—both these movements to be executed during the course of one leap. A typical step for the technical *virtuoso.*

CURTAIN